WELCOME TO THE ANCIENT OLYMPICS!

WITHDRAWN

Jane Bingham

Chicago, Illinois

Designed by Richard Parker and Tinstar Design
Illustrations by Steve Weston, Sebastian Quigley, International Mapping
Printed and bound in China by Leo Paper Group

12 11 10 09
10 9 8 7 6 5 4 3 2

Library of Congress Cataloging-in-Publication Data
Bingham, Jane.
    Welcome to the ancient Olympics! : ancient Greek Olympics / Jane Bingham.
        p. cm. -- (Fusion)
    Includes bibliographical references and index.
    ISBN-13: 978-1-4109-2889-4 (library binding - hardcover)
    ISBN-10: 1-4109-2889-6 (library binding - hardcover)
    ISBN-13: 978-1-4109-2896-2 (pbk.)
    ISBN-10: 1-4109-2896-9 (pbk.)
    1. Olympic games (Ancient)--Juvenile literature. I. Title.
    GV23.B56 2007
    796.48--dc22
                              2006039497

Acknowledgments
The publishers would like to thank the following for permission to reproduce photographs: AKG-images pp. **7** (Erich Lessing); Alamy/Visual Arts Library (London) p. **19**; Ancient Art & Architecture Collection Ltd pp. **9**, **13**, **23** (R. Sheridan), **11 17** (C.M. Dixon); The Art Archive/Archaeological Museum Florence/ Dagli Orti p. **14**; The Art Archive/National Archaeological Museum Athens/Dagli Orti p. **25**; The Art Archive/Archaeological Museum Tarquinia/Dagli Orti p. **8**; The Bridgeman Art Library/British Museum, London, U.K. p. **24**; Corbis pp. **20** (Gianni Dagli Orti), **27** (Pete Saloutos).

Cover photograph of the Statue of Discobolus in front of the Athens Stadium, Greece, reproduced with permission of Alamy/Petr Svarc.

Every effort has been made to contact copyright holders of any material reproduced in this book. Any omissions will be rectified in subsequent printings if notice is given to the publishers.

The publishers would like to thank Nancy Harris and Michael Vickers for their assistance with the preparation of this book.

Contents

Some words are printed in bold, **like this**. You can find out what they mean on page 30. You can also look in the box at the bottom of the page where they first appear.

Welcome to the Olympics!

Legend:
- Ancient Greek world
- • Some important city-states
- — Modern-day border

FRANCE

Black Sea

SPAIN

ITALY
- Kyme
- Naples
- Taranto

See enlargement

GREECE
- Athens

TURKEY

Masilia

Olbia

Cyprus

Mediterranean Sea

GREECE
- Abdera
- Delcus
- Pydna
- Assus
- Olympia — Games held here
- Athens
- Argos
- Sparta
- Miletos

0   100 Miles
0   100 Kilometers

Kyrene

Alexandria

NORTH AFRICA

EGYPT

0   150   300 Miles
0   150   300 Kilometers

The time:
400 BCE (about 2,400 years ago)

The place:
Olympia, in ancient Greece

The sporting events:
Five days of races and competitions

The religious events:
Ceremonies (special actions) for the god Zeus

The competitors:
Top athletes from the Greek world

What to bring:
Gifts for Zeus

↑ This is a map of the ancient Greek world. The countries on the map did not exist at the time of the ancient Greeks.

4

ceremony   special actions, words, and music that people perform
festival   special time of year when people meet to have
            fun and to remember an important event

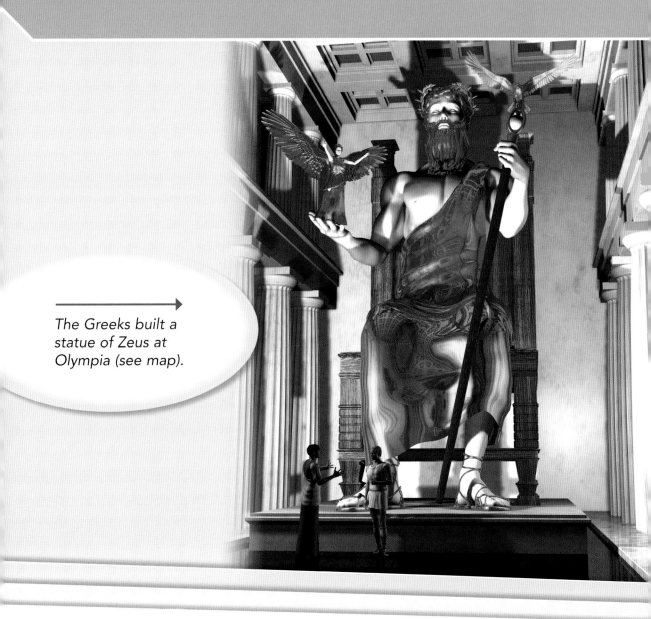

The Greeks built a statue of Zeus at Olympia (see map).

Who was Zeus?

The ancient Greeks had many gods. Zeus was their main god. The Greeks held a **festival** for Zeus at Olympia. This was an event that was held every year. This festival became the Olympic Games.

What's on at the Games?

At the ancient Olympics, there are some exciting **contests** (competitions). These might include a boxing match or a race. There are also some grand **ceremonies**. In one ceremony, competitors promise to compete with honor. They also promise to respect the rules.

Pentathlon and pankration

The **pentathlon** and the **pankration** are the toughest events. In the pentathlon, athletes compete in five different sports. In the pankration, contestants box and wrestle.

The Games at a glance

Day one: Opening ceremony and boys' events
Day two: Chariot races and pentathlon
Day three: Ceremony for Zeus and running races
Day four: Boxing, wrestling, and pankration
Day five: Prize-giving, feasts, and **celebrations**

chariot

celebration   special event to mark an important day
contest   another word for a competition
pankration   event in which athletes fought against each other. It had almost no rules.
pentathlon   Olympic event with five different sports

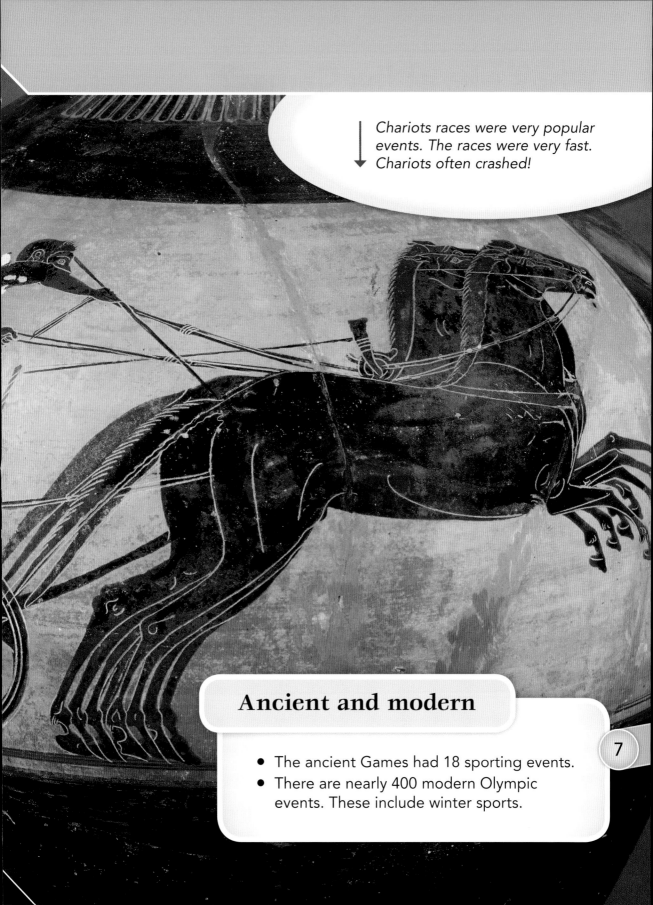

Chariots races were very popular events. The races were very fast. Chariots often crashed!

Ancient and modern

- The ancient Games had 18 sporting events.
- There are nearly 400 modern Olympic events. These include winter sports.

Who's who at the Games?

Athletes and trainers work out at Olympia. Athletes are very strong and fit. Trainers carry a long, thin stick. They use their stick to point out what the athlete is doing wrong. Sometimes they give lazy athletes a smack!

Judges and priests (religious leaders) also spend time at Olympia. Judges have purple robes. Priests often wear white. All the judges come from Olympia. But they never favor the local athletes. Olympic judges are very fair.

The trainer (right) is making sure the athlete is working hard.

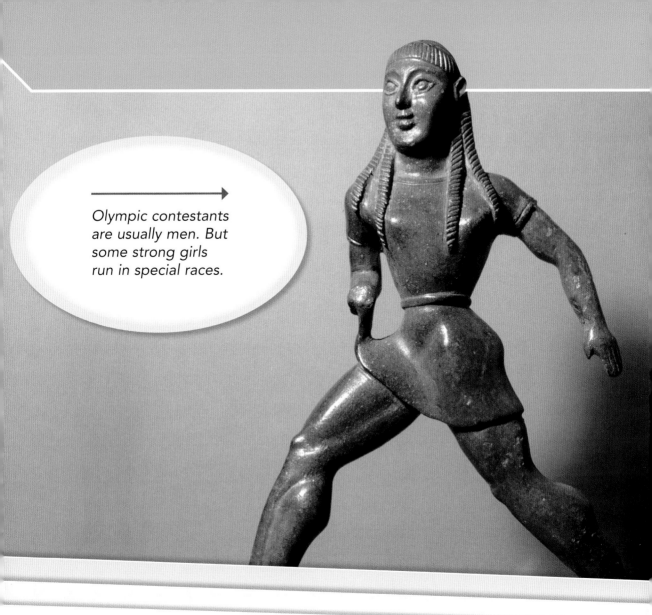

Olympic contestants are usually men. But some strong girls run in special races.

Women at the Games

There are no adult women at Olympia. Only girls can watch the Games. A married woman cannot be in the crowd. If one is found, she is thrown off a cliff!

There are a few running races for girls. These races are held in honor of Hera. She is the Greek goddess of girls and women.

Cities

People come from far away to compete. But everyone at the Games has one thing in common. All the athletes belong to a Greek **city-state**. A city-state is a large city and the farmland around it. Each one has its own ruler (leader).

Each city-state has its own athletes. There is fierce competition among the states. Athens and Sparta are the biggest rivals.

A time of peace

A few city-states are more than just sports rivals. They also fight bloody wars against each other. But all the fighting stops during the Games. For a few weeks, there is a time of peace. This is known as the **Olympic truce**.

Olympic fact!

You would not want to mess with an athlete from Sparta. Spartan babies are left out in the cold. This is to make them tough. Spartan boys and girls practice fighting every day.

city-state   large city and the farmland around it
Olympic truce   time when all wars stopped in ancient Greece

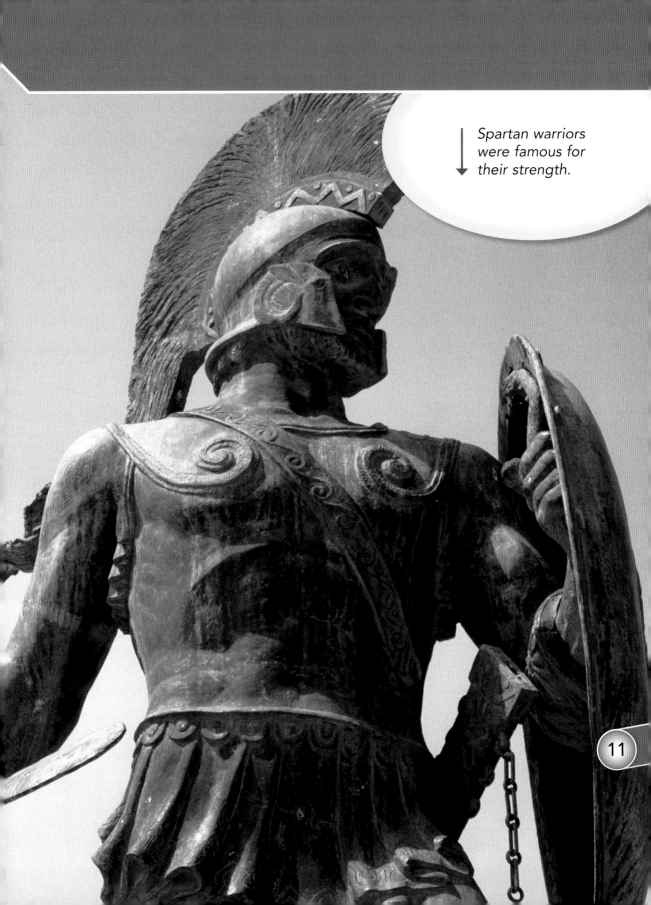

Spartan warriors were famous for their strength.

Olympia

The stadium

The stadium is a huge, rectangular area. It is surrounded by rows of seats. There are seats for about 45,000 people! Everyone in the stadium has a good view.

Some seats are made from dirt. Some are made from stone. The seats made from dirt are for anyone. The stone seats are kept for very important people.

This is a plan of how Olympia looked.

1 Temple of Hera
2 Temple of Zeus
3 The treasuries
4 The stadium
5 Athletes' center
6 The sanctuary of Zeus
7 The Palaestra

N
W—E
S

150 ft
50 m

sacred holy, or related to a religion
sanctuary very holy place
treasury place where treasure is kept

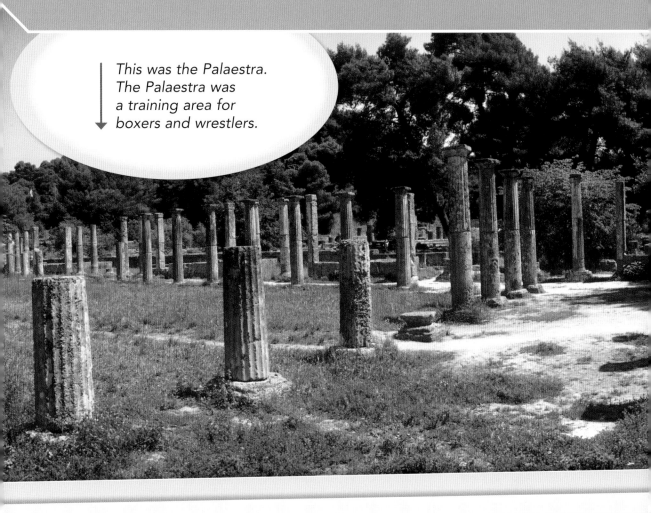

This was the Palaestra. The Palaestra was a training area for boxers and wrestlers.

The sanctuary

The **sanctuary** is a **sacred** (holy) space. The most important place is the Temple of Zeus. A temple is where people go to pray to the gods. The **treasuries** are places where gifts for Zeus are kept.

The Greeks believe that the Temple of Zeus marks a special spot. It is where Zeus threw a thunderbolt. He threw it because he was angry with the people of Earth!

Olympic Events

Three running events are held on day three. One is the stadion. This is a quick sprint down one side of the stadium. This short race covers a distance of roughly 210 yards (190 meters). The longest race of the day covers 3 miles (5,000 meters). Athletes run 12 laps of the stadium.

This Greek dish shows an Olympic runner.

Test of strength

A real test of strength comes when all the runners have to wear armor. Runners wear a helmet and leg protectors. They also carry a heavy shield. A shield was used to protect a soldier's body in battle. Athletes run four laps of the stadium. Often they collapse before the end of the race.

Men who ran in armor were usually soldiers. The race was very good training for them.

Olympic fact!

Runners in armor carry a weight of up to 55 pounds (25 kilograms). That is like carrying about 65 cans full of soda!

Boxing and wrestling

On day four there is boxing and wrestling. The athletes often get some nasty **injuries** (damage to their bodies)!

Greek boxing and wrestling are very dangerous sports. Boxers are allowed to hit an **opponent** (someone competing against them) when he is down. Wrestlers can break their opponent's fingers. Wrestlers are often covered with animal fat. The fat makes them greasy. This helps them to slip out of their opponent's grip.

The pankration

The violent **pankration** has almost no rules. Fighters are allowed to punch, bite, and scratch. They can even kick. The **contest** lasts until one fighter collapses or is killed.

Olympic fact!

In the pankration, fighters sometimes use their fingernails to rip out each other's eyes.

injury   some kind of damage or harm to your body
opponent   someone who is competing against you

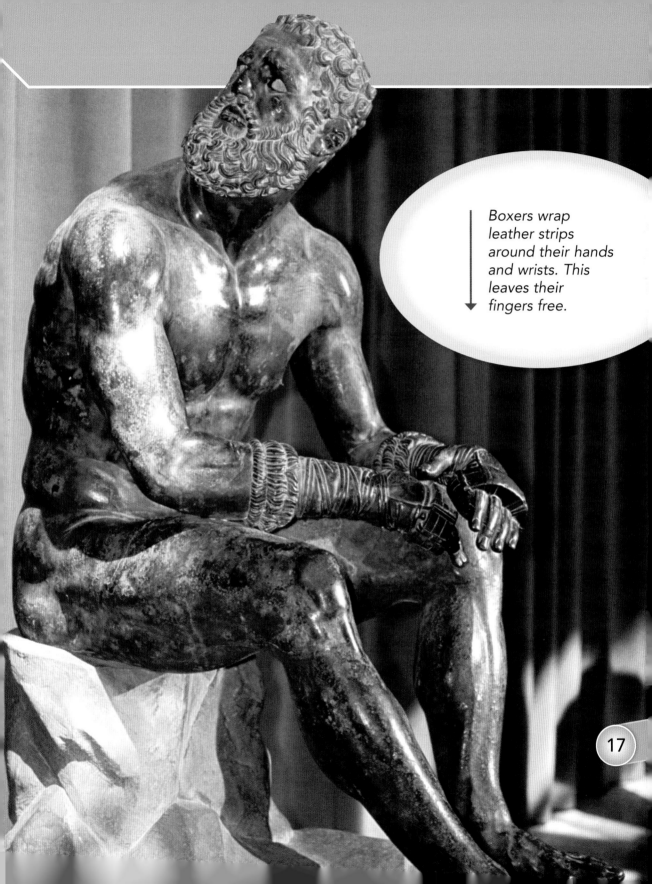

Boxers wrap leather strips around their hands and wrists. This leaves their fingers free.

The pentathlon

The **pentathlon** is made up of five sports:

- throwing the discus
- hurling the javelin
- running
- long jump
- wrestling.

Only the best athletes take part in this event.

Athletes need great strength to throw the discus and the javelin. The discus is a flat, heavy disc. It is about the size of a dinner plate. It is usually made from stone, iron, or lead The javelin is a metal-tipped wooden spear. It is as long as a man's body.

For the long jump, the athlete holds heavy stone weights. He holds a weight in each hand. First, he jumps up. He holds out the weights in front of him. Then, he comes down. He swings the weights behind him as he comes down. This helps to push him forward.

Ancient and modern

- The ancient pentathlon sports were discus, javelin, running, long jump, and wrestling.
- The modern pentathlon sports are pistol shooting, fencing, swimming, horse riding, and cross-country running.

This athlete is about to throw a discus. He is taking part in the pentathlon.

19

Ceremonies and Feasts

The Olympic Games are not just about sports. They are also an important religious event. The grand opening is very exciting.

Before the Games begin, there is a grand march. It goes to the Statue of Zeus. The athletes promise to obey the rules of the Games. They also swear that they have trained for at least 10 months.

Some athletes pray to Nike. She is the goddess of victory.

predict   tell the future
sacrifice   something that is killed and offered to the gods as a gift

Sacrifices often take place in the open air. Priests roast meat from an ox on the altar.

Honoring Zeus

On day three, everybody gathers at the Temple of Zeus.
The priest kills an ox. He looks at the animal's liver and heart.
They help him to **predict** (guess) who will win the Games.

Priests burn an ox on a large fire. The ox is a **sacrifice** to Zeus.
A sacrifice is a special gift to a god. The priests wait for the
smoke to rise to the heavens. Then, they carve up the ox meat.
They serve it to the crowd.

On Your Mark, Get Set, Go!

Olympic athletes have to train for at least 10 months. They also have to arrive four weeks early. This is for extra training at Olympia.

Olympic athletes spend many hours training. They work very hard. After they exercise they are rubbed down with oil. Then, they eat a huge meal!

Prizes and rewards

There are no money prizes at the ancient Olympics. Instead, the winner is given a simple crown. It was often made from olive leaves. Sometimes the **victor** (winner) is given ribbons. Winning athletes are treated like heroes in their home city. Sculptors make statues showing them in action. Poets write poems to praise their skill.

This athlete is a winner! He has been given ribbons as a prize.

victor   winner of a competition

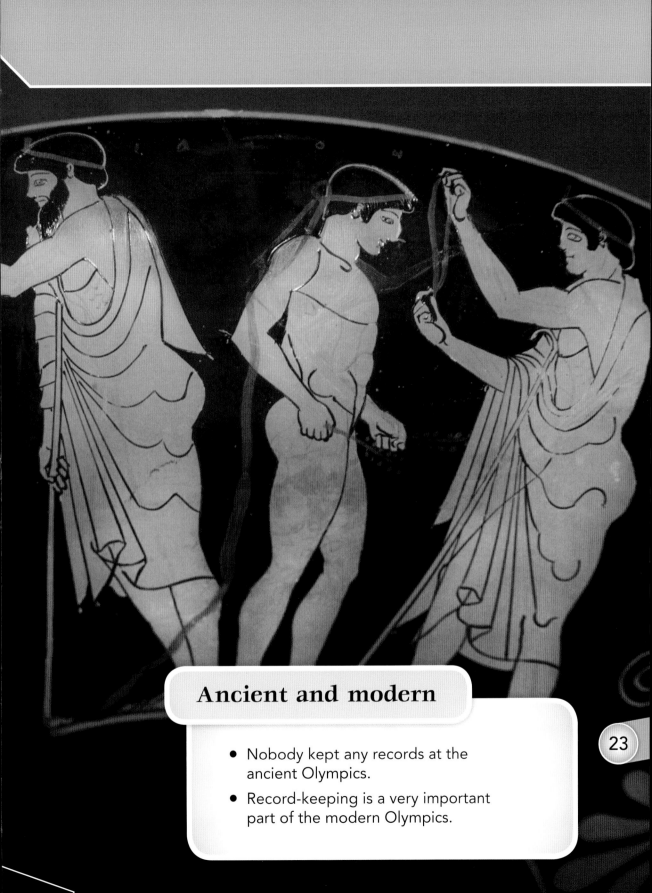

Ancient and modern

- Nobody kept any records at the ancient Olympics.
- Record-keeping is a very important part of the modern Olympics.

Olympic superstars

Some amazing people competed in the ancient Greek Olympics.
Here are just a few superstars.

Milo of Croton

Milo was a champion wrestler. He won the Olympic **victor's** crown
six times. Milo trained by lifting a calf every day. The calf grew into a
bull. Milo became very strong. Milo once saved his friends' lives. He
held up the pillar of a falling building. His friends all escaped.

Wrestlers had to be
extremely strong. ↓

↑ Boxers usually hit very hard.

Melancomas of Caria

Melancomas was a famous boxer. He had an unusual style. He liked to dodge the blows of his **opponents**. He did this instead of hitting back. Melancomas could fight all day without rest.

Aegeus of Argos

Aegeus won the long-distance race at Olympia. Then, he ran straight home to tell the people of Argos. This journey involved running nonstop for about 60 miles (96 kilometers). Aegeus ran more than twice as far as a modern marathon runner!

The Modern Olympics

The last ancient Olympics were held in 393 CE. That was about 1,600 years ago. By this time the Romans were running the Olympics. They liked more violent games. There was a gap of around 1,500 years. No Games were held.

In 1896 the first modern Games were held in Athens, Greece. This was the start of a new **series** (group) of Olympic Games.

The Olympic flame

Today, a team of **relay runners** carries a lighted torch from Olympia. The runners take it to the city where the Games are held. At the opening **ceremony**, the torch is used to light the Olympic flame. The flame burns all through the Games. The Olympic flame provides a link with the ancient (old) Olympics. During the ancient Games, a flame was kept burning in the Temple of Zeus.

relay runner   member of a running team
series   group of related things that follow each other in order

It is a great honor to
carry the Olympic torch.

The Story of the Marathon

The marathon is a running race in the modern Olympics. It covers about 26 miles (42 kilometers). The marathon was not part of the ancient Games. But it did begin in ancient Greece.

A marathon run

In 490 BCE the Greeks won a battle. It happened near the city of Marathon. The Greeks sent a messenger to Athens with the news. The messenger ran from Marathon to Athens. When he got to Athens, he cried, "Victory!" Then, he collapsed and died.

Olympic marathons

The first marathon race was run in 1896. It was an event in the first modern Olympics. Runners raced from Marathon to Athens. They covered a distance of nearly 24 miles (38 kilometers).

In 1908 the Olympics were held in London, England. The runners in the London marathon ran an extra 2 miles (3.2 kilometers). After this race, the marathon covered about 26 miles (42 kilometers).

Timeline

BCE

776

The first Olympic Games are held at Olympia. There is just one event—a short running race.

Around 720

A second running race is added to the Games. By this time the Games are held every four years.

632

The Olympics last for five days.

393

The Games are officially ended by Roman Emperor Theodosius. This is the end of the ancient Olympics.

1924

The first Winter Olympics are held at Chamonix, France.

1960

The first Paralympics are held for athletes with physical disabilities.

2008

The Olympics are held in Beijing, China.

2012

The Olympic Games will be held in London.

CE

1894

The International Olympic Committee (IOC) is founded.

1896

The first modern Olympics are held in Athens, Greece. Many new sports, including the marathon, are introduced.

1900

Women are allowed to take part in the Games.

Glossary

celebration special event to mark an important day. Birthday parties are celebrations.

ceremony special actions, words, and music that people perform. Some ceremonies are held in honor of a god.

city-state large city and the farmland around it. In ancient Greece there were several city-states.

contest another word for a competition. You can take part in a swimming contest or a running contest, for example.

festival special time of year when people meet to have fun and to remember an important event.

injury some kind of damage or harm to your body. Injuries can be minor, like a sore finger, or very serious, like a broken neck.

Olympic truce time when all wars stopped in ancient Greece. During the truce everyone could enjoy the Olympic Games.

opponent someone who is competing against you. Opponents can be friendly or fierce.

pankration event in which athletes fought against each other. It had almost no rules. In the modern Olympics the pankration would be banned.

pentathlon Olympic event with five different sports. The pentathlon of the ancient Olympics was very different from the modern pentathlon event.

predict tell the future. A priest predicted who would win the Games.

relay runner member of a running team. Each relay runner runs for part of the way before the next team member takes over.

sacred holy, or related to a religion. Many religions have sacred places and sacred music.

sacrifice something that is killed and offered to the gods as a gift.

sanctuary very holy place. The word *sanctuary* can also mean a safe place, as in an animal sanctuary.

series group of related things that follow each other in order. The new series of Olympic Games began in 1896.

treasury place where treasure is kept. Another name for treasury is *treasure house*.

victor winner of a competition. Sometimes people use the word *victor* to mean the winner of a battle.

Want to Know More?

Books to read

Gaff, Jackie. *Ancient Olympics*. Chicago: Heinemann Library, 2004.

Osborne, Mary Pope, and Natalie Pope Boyce. *Ancient Greece and the Olympics*. New York: Random House, 2004.

Websites

www.socialstudiesforkids.com/articles/worldhistory/ancientgreekolympics1.htm
Learn more about the ancient Olympics at this site.

www.perseus.tufts.edu/olympics/
This site includes sections on Olympia, famous athletes, and the different events at the Games.

www.historyforkids.org/learn/greeks/games/olympics.htm
This website takes a look at the ancient Olympic Games.

Read more about the ancient Romans in ***Staying Alive in Ancient Rome***.

Read more about the people of ancient Egypt in ***Reach for the Stars***.

Index